Survival Communication:

20 Best Survival Skills To Stay In-Touch With Your Family During The Disaster

Table of content:

Introduction.

Emergency communication must be one of your top priorities in an emergency disaster scenario. The ability to receive or to send information could mean the difference between you and your loved ones surviving or not.

Many of us do not realize this fact, but whenever you transmit a message through any device that is connected to the communication infrastructure, you are taking an inherent risk.

There are thousands of hackers in the United States alone working all day to steal as much data as they possibly can, ranging from a single hacker in the basement to well organized criminal groups.

Each time you use a modern form of communication, whether it be your smart phone, your tablet, your laptop, your email, the internet, or even social media, there is a perfectly good chance that at some point your information will become compromised.

Even though some of the communication methods we will discuss in this chapter rely on electricity, they do not rely on phone networks that the internet and phone companies provide to you.

It has been proven, time after time, that our modern communication infrastructure is extremely vulnerable to even the smallest or shortest of disasters.

Cell networks become overwhelmed, cell towers are taken offline, and so on. The simple fact of the matter is that our communication infrastructure is not designed to handle emergencies.

And yet the vast majority of Americans living today are incredibly reliant on their mobile devices. They don't realize just how ineffective these devices are going to be during a disaster.

Widespread damage to cellular infrastructure was inflicted in the summer of 2012 as storms swept through the mid-Atlantic alone, and a larger scale catastrophe means that the entire country could be affected.

When these disasters take place, people will be unable to use their phones to access the internet or to call for help through 911.

Chapter 1. Prepare a Survival Communication Plan In Advance

It is vital to make sure that your whole family is ready and conversant within the event of a disaster or emergency. You cannot always be along with themwhen these events happen therefore you should have plans to face such kind of disasters and emergencies. Also make sure that you're able to contact and find each other. Don't forget your pets in whole of the situation. They will be more worried than you. Here is how you can get mentally equipped for such an unfortunate event;

Prepare Yourself:

Before anyone else, prepare yourself to face any kind of disaster or emergency. Remember that you are going to survive the situation only if you are well planned and ready ahead of the event. There are certain steps that you can take in such a situation. Let's have a look;

Before a Disaster:

According to the American Red Cross, you must be taking the following steps in any of such events; Have a meeting with your family and household members.

Discuss and decide the type of disasters and emergencies you are expecting to face in such a situation.

Get prepared accordingly.

Assign responsibilities among all the available members.

If any of the family members is in army then decide how you will carry out things if he or she gets deployed.

During the Disaster:

If you get separated: You can get separated from your family members and friends and fellows during a disaster. This happens very commonly.

Here is what you should do if you get separated from the closed ones during a state of emergency: • Decide two places to meet, for instance, • Exactly outside your home in case of a fire.

• Outside your neighborhood if you are unable to return to your home or have been asked to evacuate.

• Select a person to contact who resides outside the area of disaster.

You can text or call him from your mobile phone or through internet if the local phone lines have gotten out of service or are overloaded. It is important to keep emergency contact information saved in your phone or written in a diary.

• If you are asked to evacuate: You can also be asked to evacuate in the cases of emergencies and disasters. In that case, take the following steps; • Select the place where you would go in such a situation.

Also decide the route through which you will reach at your safe haven. You can choose a motel or you can decide to stay with your friends or some family members living outside the area of the disaster. You can also opt for an evacuation shelter in case you don't find any other place to go instantly.

It may sound crazy but practice to evacuate. Yes! Practice to evacuate your home at least twice a year. After evacuation, drive to your destination through a specified route. Also mark other alternative routes on your map to reach the destination in case the original or the shortest one is impassable.

Also plan for your pets. Keep a list ready of the pet friendly hotels or rest houses or animal shelters or any living place which is ready to welcome your pets along with you on your evacuation route.

Inform your family and friends about your safe arrival at the destination.

Satellite Phone

Even if the phone networks collapse, a satellite phone will still work flawlessly. The reason why is because satellite phones do not use the networks that normal phones do.

How satellite phones work instead is they bounce a signal to a satellite before connecting to the device that you want to talk to.

Satellite phones are therefore great for two kinds of disasters:

1.   A Wilderness Survival Situation
2.   A Large Scale Urban Disaster

Granted, satellite phones are quite expensive, but they will also be a very wise investment because you can maintain contact with your friends, relatives, and the outside world even if the cell service towers are no longer working.

Chapter 2.Best Survival Radios

Walkie-Talkie

We should all be familiar with this one. The walkie-talkie, also known as the two-way radio, is an excellent way for you to maintain verbal communication with others (though within a limited range), because it uses a non-phone network.

While the range of walkie-talkie vary by the model, most can allow you to communicate with people from thirty-five up to fifty miles.

Walkie-talkies are also dirt cheap, easily accessible, easy to store and carry, use a wide number of channels, and have a long battery life.

A large variety of different types of walkie-talkie set with wild features are available in your local market. Here we are discussing types of walkie-talkies in respect to their features;

Walkie-talkie with Far Reaching Transmission.

Not all details provided in the manuals of the walkie-talkie sets are right in their origin. Therefore, don't believe instantly on all of the information written in the sales literature when selecting a set for your disaster kit. The reason is that the distance calculated by the manufacturers is usually measured in an area with vacuum and sound travels faster and farther in vacuum. But in an area with buildings, trees, traffics and other interferences it is not possible for you to achieve the exact results. Two types of radios can help in this scenario. One is FRS *i.e.* Family Radio Service and the other is GMRS *i.e.* General Mobile Radio Service.

Walkie-talkie with Multiple Radio Channels.

Multiple radio channels are usually available in cities. Many are allotted to different areas already. Similarly, a business might have allotted different radio channels for different business functions. Whatever the case is, decide how many channels you want your radio to have especially when you intend to add in your preparedness for a disaster kit. It is crucial. Most of the walkie-talkies are either FRS or GMRS that shows that use multiple channels, for instance, GMRC uses channels from number 15 to 22.

An important point to remember is that many walkie-talkie sets also offer privacy codes. These codes can block you outside chatter on a specific channel. Further remember that the calls are not private and anyone can listen to them. the only privacy you get is that your calls cannot be interrupted by anyone.

Walkie-talkies with Batteries.

Walkie-talkie run on batteries as this feature makes them portable. It is important to know the kind of batteries that the new addition in your disaster kit is going to need for power supply. These radios come with a large variety of power supply options. Some of them use AA or AAA regular alkaline batteries that are disposable while others might be using rechargeable batteries. Remember that in a disaster, there might be no electricity supply available for you to charge your Walkie-talkie sets and once, the rechargeable battery is out, you will be out as well. Therefore, buy walkie-talkie sets with disposable batteries and also stock such batteries in your emergency kit so you don't run out of power supply anytime during the disaster. Also don't install batteries in your set while it is just kept placed in your kit because batteries automatically drain on being kept in the device for too long.

Good warranty, compatibility of the set with other devices and the handiness of the users must also be kept in mind along with the number of supported channels, distance coverage and type of power supply sources while buying walkie-talkie radios for your emergency kit. Technology evolves everyday therefore also check for new available options too.

CB Radios

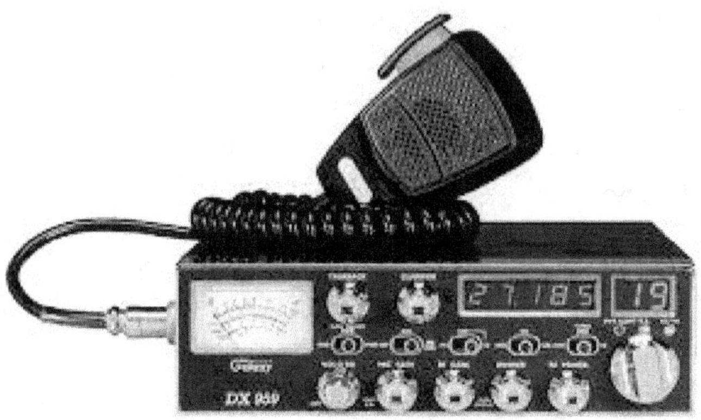

CB radios are most commonly used today by truckers, and will be a reasonable choice for a catastrophe scenario.

The biggest limitation to the CB radio is its limited range (generally no more than ten to fifteen miles). Therefore, it is only a short-range communication device and must be treated as such, but it will still work even if your smart or cell phone does not.

We will talk about CB radios in greater depth and the various codes there are for them later in this book when we talk about the best radios for you to own for survival.

Ham Radio

The ham radio is widely favored by many survivalists and with good reason. Military, law enforcement, and search-and-rescue teams also widely utilize the ham radio because of the fact that it can be used even when cell phones cannot and they have a wide range.

Ham radios also feature a scanner that will allow you to keep yourself up-to-date on what's happening in your area.

You do need a license to get a ham radio, and we'll discuss how to acquire this license later in this book. Along with that, we'll discuss ham radios in greater depth too.

Army Radio

If Walkie-talkies are no longer available, then you might have access to a much lesser used technology amongst civilians. I remember fondly the time that my father showed me his military issued radio and this thing was massive. We're talking about a big green box with an antenna that was twice the height of my body when I was seven years old. The beauty is that this type of technology is no longer only held by the military and you can go to a "military shop" to purchase one. This type of shop isn't particularly called a military shop but it is where you can buy semi-automatic weapons, camo, and other "military" gear. These radios are a bit unwieldy to say the least but perhaps that's what makes them durable. You will need to read the user manual for this.

Amateur Radio

You can get licensed to operate your own HAM radio and there is a clear distinction between regular radio and a Home Amateur Radio. Depending on your level of clearance, you can get anywhere from communicating with boats on the sea and other HAM radio operators to military personnel and helicopters. Needless to say, if you were trying to use this to communicate with loved ones then they would need to be certified anyway.

Citizens Band Radio

However, that isn't the only type of radio that's out there and this means you can target something that's normally referred to as CB radio, which is a long-distance radio channel meant for citizens. This is the type of radio that's often utilized by truckers and the police. Please understand that CB radio only has a mile radius of up to 100 miles at maximum, so you are not likely going to be able to contact people who are far off. Just so you know, the most common place to mount this device is inside of your car (hence the popularity with truckers and drivers) because you can usually keep in constant contact with anyone in your city. Most cities don't even span the total of 50 miles, so you are likely going to be able to contact anyone you need to in the city that you live in and considering most cities are nowhere near 100 miles of each other, you will find it is handy for emergency contacts inside of your car if you get stuck on a backroad of some sort. I'm honestly surprised that this don't come standard issue with our cars... we might not have so many horror movies.

Marine Band Radio

Additionally, if you're a boat operator then you might also know about the MB radio or Marine Band radio, meant for anyone travelling on the open waters. This is extremely useful for most boats out at low waters of the sea. This is a short-range radio (most of the time) and is good for many things, such as when you get lost or asking other fishermen where good fishing holes are for the day. Having said that, all the previous radios mentioned in this chapter require that you both have one so it's important that you both go down that road together or else it will be next to useless unless you can find someone nearby that will be able to receive and relay your messages.

GMRS Radios

GMRS radios are a good choice for communication in a survival situation for a number of reasons:

- They are more popular than CB radios
- Easy to use/user friendly
- Cheap and easy to get
- Do not require an FCC license

That being said, GMRS radios also have a number of limitations, especially in regard to their range and power. If you can tap into a repeater, however, then you will be able to increase your range by several hundred miles. Otherwise, your range is going to be pretty limited similar to a walkie-talkie.

Chapter 3. Flares

A flare permits you to contact others from long distances for help and are a clear sign that you are in trouble.

Flares are universally accepted as a signal of distress, so if you shoot a flare into the sky, anybody within your general area who sees it will come to your aid.

Smoke Signaling

Signaling for help with smoke is another great way to communicate with others, even if it is rather primitive.

The best way to create an effective and highly visible smoke is to select a clearing on the top or side of the hill. Burn green brush so white smoke is created that will be more visible.

You can also send specific messages with the aid of a blanket. What you need to do is soak your blanket in water so it will not burn. Then you throw your blanket over the fire until no more smoke is traveling upward.

You will then pull the blanket back to send a puff of white smoke into the air, and then throw it back over the fire.

Here are the universal signals and their meaning when communicating with smoke:

- One Puff: means there is no danger or need for alarm, but whoever you are signaling needs to stay on the lookout for future signals.

- Two Puffs: means everything is going smoothly and your camp has been safely established. All is well and it is safe to proceed.

- Three Puffs: means there is danger and cause for alarm; enemies may be approaching. Either come to aid or evacuate the area.

Alternatively, you can send an SOS message with smoke signaling. The universal SOS message is three short beats, three long beats, and then three short beats.

So in the case of smoke signaling, you would do three quick puffs rapidly together, three long puffs, and then three more quick rapid puffs.

Signal Mirror

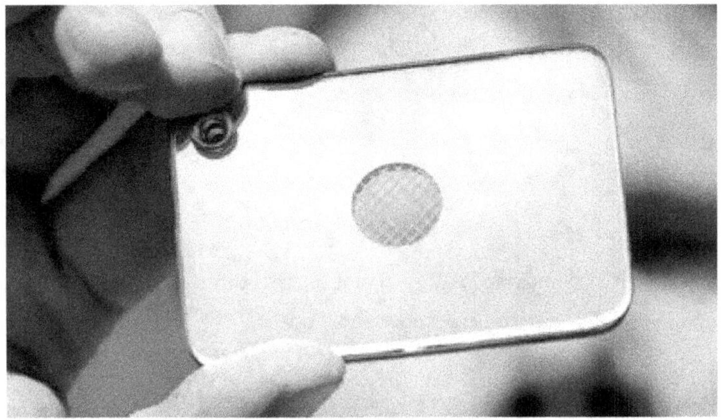

You can also communicate or request aid with a signal mirror. On a clear sunny day, you simply use your mirror to reflect the light of the sun and signal for help.

In the event that you lack a mirror, you can also use a beer or soda can and polish the bottom with chocolate to make it more reflective. You could also use the bottom reflective surface of a CD or DVD.

It's extremely easy to use a signaling mirror as well. Just follow these steps:

1.   Bring the mirror to your eye

2.   Make sure that the surface of the mirror is not obscured by your fingers or hat

3.   Tilt the mirror toward the sun

4.   You should now see a small beam of light

5.   Move the beam of light toward your target

Simple, right?

You can also send an SOS message with a signal mirror: three short light flashes, three long light flashes, and then three more short ones.

Social Media: Twitter, Instagram and Google+

I put these in the same category because they kind of come after the Facebook or email option because of their purpose. Sure, nowadays we use Twitter to display rebellions and to get almost immediate access to information because of how small each tweet is but that doesn't mean that people think of Twitter or even Instagram first in terms of contacting their loved ones during an emergency and so that's why we've listed it in the slightly less obvious category. Needless to say, Google+ is also here due to the fact that almost no one actually uses Google+ anymore but it still exists as a Google feature.

Asking a Police Officer

As much as the news in the media like to portray police officers, police officers pretty much run the behind-the-scenes network when it comes to communication within an emergency. If you go to a police officer, that's not busy, they are likely to assist you in whatever way you need because you are a person who is seeking help from a police officer. It's not really their job to do this but most police officers will do things that are not necessarily required of them simply because they got into their job because they love helping people or they like the feeling of being needed. This means that if you ask them to get a message to your loved one then they would be able to use their resources to ensure that your message gets sent. It's slightly less obvious, but it's nowhere near as advanced as some of the things we'll discuss here.

Using a Pay Phone

At this point it's kind of like I'm talking about a dinosaur when I talk about a pay phone because most people hear the option of going and utilizing a pay phone and then they begin to question whether those devices even exist anymore or even what the device is, depending on how young that individual is. The truth is that they are a legal mandate by the city and so while they did remove a giant portion of public phones from cities around the United States of America, that doesn't mean that they removed the all. The truth of the matter is that you are more likely to find a payphone inside of downtown then you are if you're outside of downtown because downtown is where the most collected amount of individuals are that would be able to benefit from the use of a pay phone. You see, even though the pay phone is legally mandated they still put it in places where it makes sense to keep maintenance on the machine as low as possible.

Chapter 4. Light-Safe Signals

Here's another one for the individuals trying to communicate with the other individuals across the street. This type of technique involves you having a flashlight and the individual you're trying to contact having a flashlight. Essentially, all you want to do is you want to flash a light twice to see if they are alright and wait for the other person to flash once to say that they are okay. It takes the purpose of the conversation between two neighborhood houses and reduces it to the core reasons of why the two of you are conversing in the first place. However, that doesn't mean that you can't go any further than that because if you learn how to send out Morse code and you teach the other individual how to send out Morse code, the two of you can begin to talk to each other with flashlights without even needing a cell phone or a walkie-talkie because Morse code was the original form of long range electronic translation. Morse code isn't that difficult to implement either because you simply wait for the start of a sequence of blinks and non-blinks and then once that sequence is over, you write down either a word or a phrase or a character. Either way, once you rinse and repeat this action of few tens to hundreds of times, you are then able to connect it all together and read the entirety of the material in the safe place that is your home.

Google Voice Texting

There are some obscure parts of Google and this is important to understand because there are services like Google Voice and Google Hangouts. If your cell phone doesn't work but you can get in contact with Google Voice and if your cell phone is attached to a cellular plan, you can call people from Google Voice. You can also text them if you need to because Google Voice gives you the option of having a secondary number and the most common secondary number that they have for most people trying to use Google Voice is a Texas number. I keep Google Voice around for when the going gets tough, it's great to have a secondary plan where I can contact people with something other than my cellular device because it's not like people expect mail today.

That's not the only limitation that comes with Google Voice though because you also have the fact that if you do not have any cellular number attached to a cellular plan and you attempt to call an individual through Google Voice without having one, it will direct you to the default phone line and then you will be blocked. In some cases, you can actually mitigate this and get it to read as the Google Voice number in your account but you have to have a specific type of phone in order to achieve this. It's really just easier to make sure that you have a cellular plan attached to your phone in case of an emergency but it is useful in texting people because it doesn't deny you access to that if you don't have a cellular plan.

Google Hangouts

Google Hangouts is a software that has been around for quite a bit of time but didn't gain as much traction as Skype or SnapChat or any of the other video based messengers and this is because Google didn't really do a good job selling their software. That doesn't mean that it's going to be the most popular in the market but it does have one feature that's very useful in case of an emergency and I don't mean a 911 emergency but just contacting your relatives emergency. You see, if you decide that you want to set up a Google Voice account and get a number, that number will be registered to your Google Hangouts account. Once the number is registered to your Google Hangouts account, you can then begin to expect to be able to call individuals over Google Hangouts in the web browser and I find that this is very useful as a backup cell phone whenever I don't have a cellular plan and I make sure that all of my family members are aware that this number exists. Now I will say that this is kind of limited because if you trying to contact anyone that's outside of the US, it's going to cost you money but as long as you're calling people inside of America then you're usually going to have a phone call free of charge. This is because Google utilizes its own VoIP system in order to allow people to not only contact individuals over the phone but also contact individuals over the internet.

Send A Text Via "send-a-text" Technology

Google voice isn't the only place where you can send out text messages and this is very important to understand because there is a difference. Google Voice gives you a phone number and this phone number can be saved inside of the contacts list of your loved ones, which means that they won't block you or their service provider won't block you whenever you try to contact them. With that said, if you don't mind not having a recognizable phone number, then you can go with a secondary option if you prefer not set up a Google Voice account and that is to send text with websites that will send texts for you. Normally, you just type in the website and then type in the text along with where the phone number is and hit send in order to send out your text. This is actually a technology that's been around for almost a decade or two that a lot of people in the First World countries simply don't know about because why would you need to know about it if you have a cell phone plan in the first place. Certain job opportunities provide you with the ability to be in a country are there are no cell phones and this becomes extremely problematic whenever you need to send text messages and produce phone calls and the only thing that you have is the internet. Not only that, but the internet is watched. This is why it's very useful to have such technology that can provide you with the cellular services that you need on a connection that you didn't expect it.

Using A Walmart Laptop

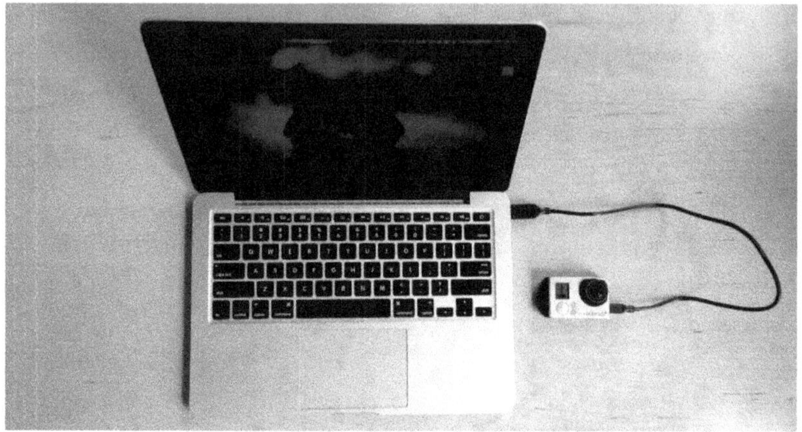

Ironically, whenever most people say that they can't do the previous two, their reasoning is that they have no access to a computer and this is funny because of how wrong the thought processes are. Why would anyone buy a computer that they didn't test it first? This is a tested and tried rule when it comes to products. A customer doesn't care about what a giant list of hardware specifications say about the hardware but just that the hardware works in the way that they expected. In order to do that with computers, items that literally costs hundreds of dollars, most stores allow the computers being sold to be displayed on a shelf that can then be used. This means that the customer not only has access to a computer but, most of the time, because they primarily test for speed in the browser, they also have internet access on the computer so if you don't have a phone and don't even have a computer to utilize the tools I just gave you, you can actually go to one of these stores and use their computer for a quick second to utilize the tools I just gave you, but that doesn't mean that this doesn't come with limitations.

First of all, remember that the computer is not yours. You may be using the computer but the computer is not yours and so you have to be respectful of the company where the computer is stored at and you have to understand that some businesses do not connect it to the internet but most do.

Therefore, you are taking a risk at this point. However, in case of an emergency you can utilize this as a last-ditch effort to contact an individual that you may need assistance from. However, if you are so desperate that you need to go to the Walmart down the road so that you can use computers on their display, then I highly suggest you go talk to a police officer if you can. If the world is ending, don't expect the internet to be up for more than a few weeks. It takes a lot of manpower to keep the internet running.

Using Desktop IM

Since we're on the aspect of utilizing desktops and laptops in order to send out messages, this springs up the instant messenger that people used to use and have on their desktops. You see, for every language that there is on the planet there's likely a chat system that can be geared specifically towards that language.

This means that if you give it enough time, you will eventually find any chat system that is specifically built for your language and your needs. You have to realize that before people had text messaging on their phones, they had instant messenger via AOL or some other service on their desktop. This means that they have had more time to develop software packages for desktop instant messengers than they have had cell phones.

Needless to say, you will need to have the other individual sign up to this beforehand but it is a good option to have these types of technologies available on hand if you just so happen to get into a binding spot where you need to use these to contact whoever you're trying to contact over to the other side.

Chapter 5. Online Chat Rooms

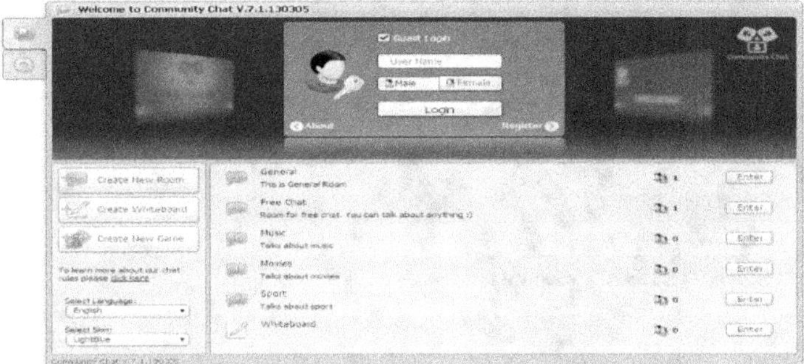

Another Advanced option is a command line trap room. You do have online websites where you can just go in and randomly chat with a user but there are still command line chat rooms and the reason why this is a more advanced version is because this is usually referred to as a relay chat. A relay chat takes identified nodes on a network and connect them so that they relay messages to each other, which is why it was one of the very first methods of creating a chat system. You can use someone else's relay chat system and set this up on everyone's computer or you can create your own with some digging in a little research, but the honest truth is that an online relay chat room is capable of working on any device that receives a internet connection.

As odd as it may seem, landline phones are still in use and a lot of people find it rather on that one of the main advices for people is to get a landline phone in case of an emergency because they don't understand why you would need such a device if you have a cell phone. However, you have to realize that the landline phone was built to withstand some incredible stuff and it was also built in a very unique way. If you truly have a landline phone and not something that requires auxiliary power but the landline phone that just accepts the phone line, you will be able to run that phone whenever the power is out because the power that the landline phone receives comes from the phone line itself. This is incredibly ingenious but also something that many people seem to forget whenever they go to buy their smartphone and don't see a landline phone as something being needed.

The Spark Gap Transmitter:

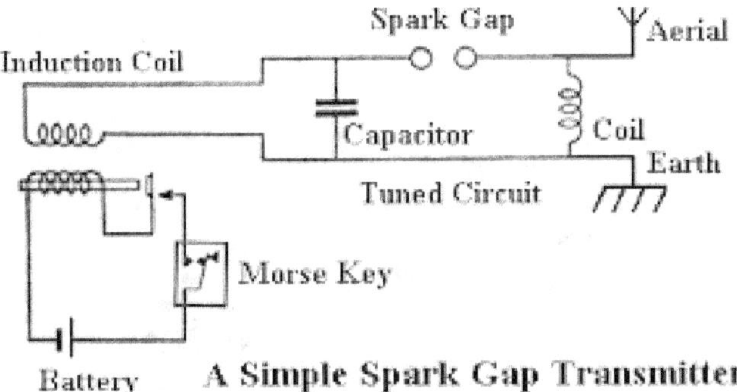

A Simple Spark Gap Transmitter

The spark gap transmitters were first used in 1800 and literally the first device to be used for radio transmission. These transmitters work by generating spark across a spark gap in the transmitter. Their advantage is that they are easily manufactured and are easily used. They have a huge range working over a number of frequencies and also as a back-up for distress messages on the international distress frequency of 500 kHz (600 meters) right up to the beginning of World War II.

The thing make its use is illegal, is its range. Also transmission of signals and understanding them require expertise as the messages transmitted can only be understood if the person knows the Morse code or they have their own transmission code to interpret what is being said.

Repeaters:

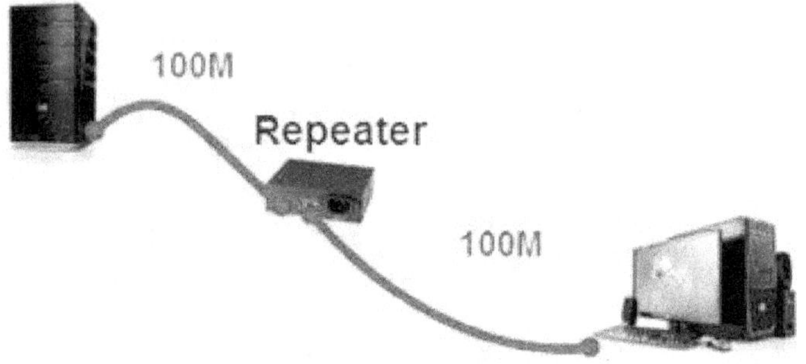

A repeater is a device which can transmit signals repeatedly to increase its power so it could be heard at a longer distance as during transmission much power is lost in term of heat or electric current. A repeater consists of a radio receiver, an amplifier, a transmitter, an isolator, and two antennas. They omit the nuisance during a transmission making signals and sound clear. There are a lot of people around the corner using repeaters as a mean of communication. They carry signals from radios in its surrounding and increase its power to be heard at a longer distance. People who use repeaters are on emergency communication and keep backup power as they use an external source of power.

The internet does have repeaters. All you need is to click repeater option and have to write the address of another person using a repeater and what you will be saying over your radio can be heard on the other side of the hand.

Art can be life-saving in case of a disaster. Only a spray paint can give a clue about the route of the exit of a person or family who can later be rescued. Family members can be taught about different signals or signs distinct to a particular condition and understood by only specific family members. These practices can be made friendly and joyful as well can be fed in memory of every family member if planned as a game adventure. Not only sign and signals can help to trace but also writing text message directly that "I went to that place, or that way" can be used but these direct clues could alert an unknown person who should not get aware of the location.

The most appropriate way are signs and symbols only known by family members should be used. There could be a possible situation when a wife does not reach home on time, and there is no way to contact. Husband can trace her by following her regular or alternate route to the home where a private message in terms of sign or signal can be found and can reunite the couple without wasting time in unavailing search and suffering others.

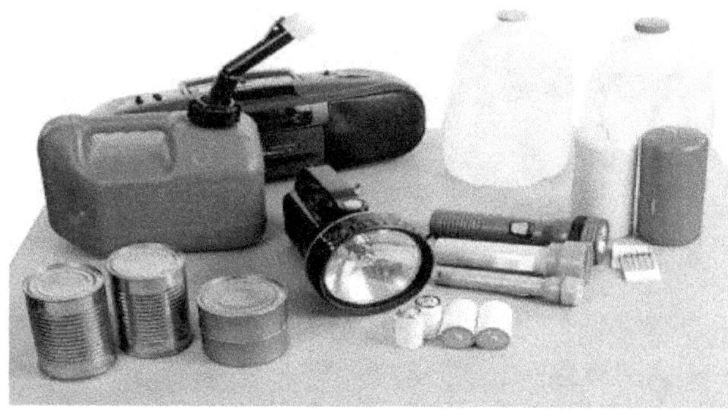

Caches are the substances which are same in type and are stored in unreachable places. Different types of caches can be located at various places only known by family members as trace. These can be placed from school to home or workplace to home at every possible path. These not only provide a trace of the path but also play a role as hidden message and meeting point to reunite. The path of cache needs to skillfully plan out even if it's of short distance covering few miles so that in the case of emergency it can easily be followed.

Hidden messages can be given by placing them in the caches that could be in the form of a pen, paper, painted cans, symbols or simply written message. These messages can serve to re-locate family members, change of plan or meeting point. Any information about personal location can bring about a mental and emotional relief to family members who get separated in any sort of atrocity.

The maps about the track of caches should be placed bags, get me home bags, and especially in the children's backpacks and children should be known to these places and those should be approachable at the time of need.

In case if the caches are being lost or hidden by a delinquent so there should be emergency caches. These emergency caches serve as ultimate approach retrieve communication and uniting family members once they have been separated.

Conclusion

Effective communication truly is one of the best survival skills that you can learn. The very act of being able to get a hold of your relatives to send and receive information will be invaluable and potentially lifesaving.

What you need to do is you need to develop a family emergency communications plan, and you need to confirm that everybody in your family knows the plan (this is why practicing the plan will come in handy).

It's not likely that everyone in your family is going to be together when disaster strikes: your kids could be in school or visiting friends, you could be at work or running errands, and so on.

This is why you must absolutely have a firm plan in place to ensure that everyone in your family can find each other during the emergency situation.

Thank you for purchasing this book; it is my sincere hope that you will apply the required knowledge productively.

www.ingramcontent.com/pod-product-compliance
Lightning Source LLC
Chambersburg PA
CBHW070746260726
48660CB00007B/3002